Evaluation Illustrated

This is not an evaluation textbook.

A book of cartoons by Chris Lysy

freshspectrum

For Jen and Mady, the two most important people in my life. Your love & support has meant everything.

Does anyone else feel like we could do better?

Introduction

Many of the evaluators I know are pragmatic dreamers. They can be hopeful and idealistic, but they approach their work systematically and realistically. They work in an often political field that is filled with contradictions and ethical challenges. They get put into positions that can feel lonely but also incredibly important.

I started drawing cartoons in 2011, at which point I had just recently found my way into the field of evaluation. For most of the previous decade I was a sociologist working as a social science researcher.

My cartooning followed along with my understanding of this new-to-me field. I never expected my cartoons would find such an amazing audience. Or that I would have fans of my work willing to buy a book like this one.

I am no Charles Schultz, Scott Adams, or Randall Monroe. While my illustrations have gotten better, I still plan to keep my day job.

For this book I decided to keep the cartoons in their original formats. Even the early ones that feel like scribbles. The illustration quality is not all that great, but the ideas behind the cartoons hold strong.

Finally, I want to thank all of the evaluators who continue to share my work in presentations, social media postings, websites, reports, and books. Your support keeps me motivated.

For royalty-free downloads of all the cartoons in this book, visit https://freshspectrum.com/evaluation-illustrated

The real question is "what isn't evaluation?"

So there are these birds and bees and...

Is your husband giving the talk?

No, the kids just asked him what he does as an evaluator

I can't tell you
how valuable
your program is

I can

Researcher

Evaluator

At the beginning of every evaluation

I know our
project works

No,
you don't

Uh oh, it looks like our evaluator is coming to chat about our project performance.

We hired you, your job is to report what we say.

You did hire me, but as an evaluator that's not my job.

This is our evaluator. Every time she collects data it will help us remember what we said we were going to do in the first place.

What kind of evaluation did you need?

Our 3 year project is coming to an end and were told we needed an evaluation.

What kind is that?

At the logic model repair shop ...

So, I'm guessing this is for a comprehensive program-level intervention

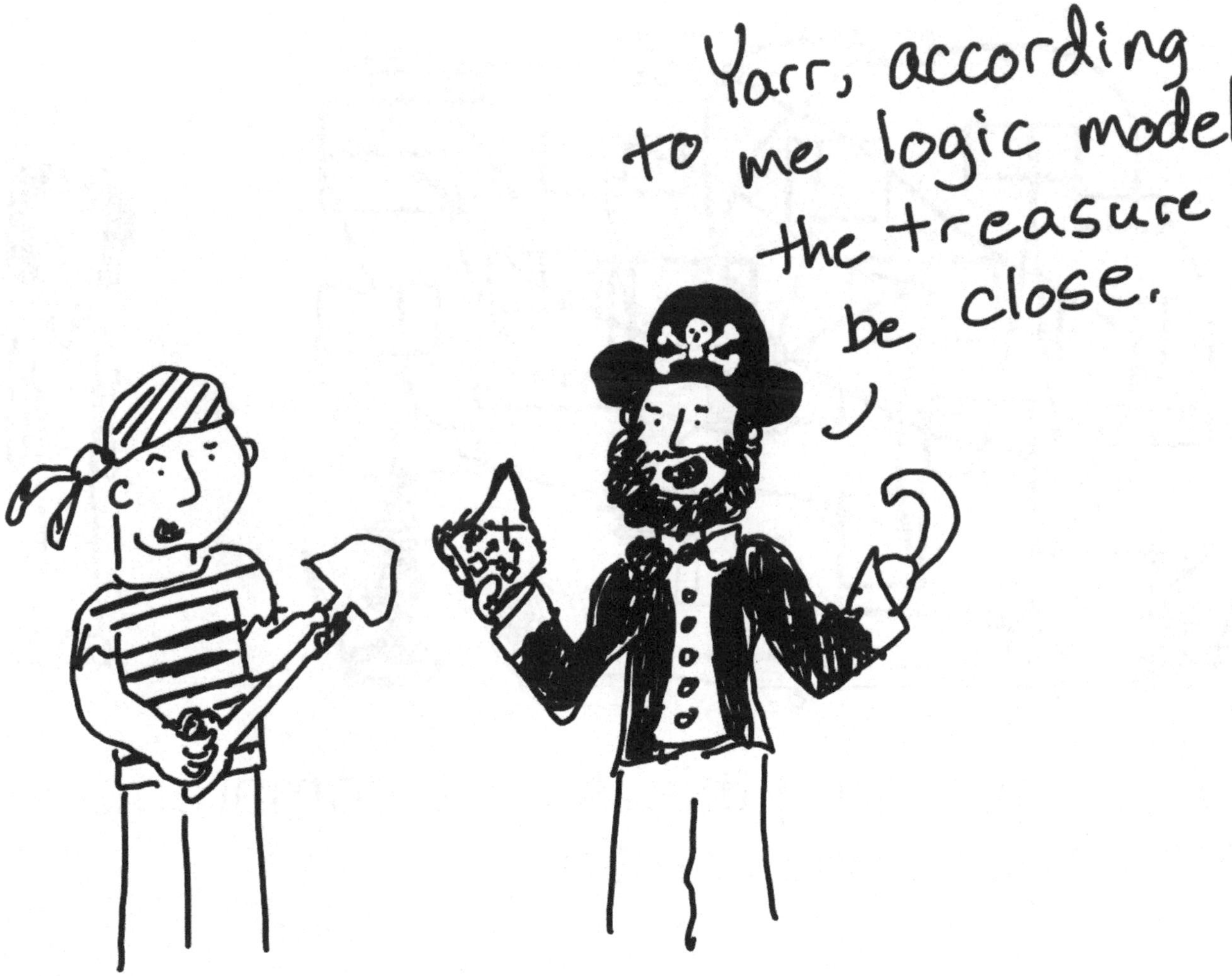
Yarr, according to me logic model the treasure be close.

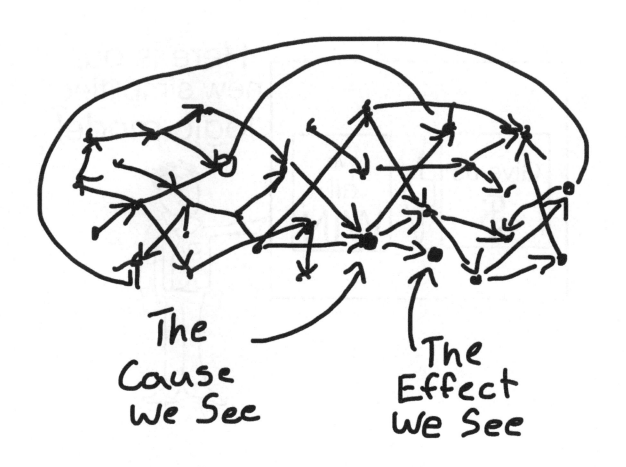

The
Cause
We See

The
Effect
We See

Logic Model Tip: Models do not need to be drawn to scale

Now if you'll follow me into the next room,
we'll take a look at some of the long term outcomes

16

You're right, after thinking it through,
I'm not sure how the one leads to the other

We have limited resources so I'm going to suggest we only fund projects that work really well.

Hi, I donated $20 last year.
Can you tell me exactly how many
Children I've saved?

And that's when I had my aha moment. We don't have to prove the program works. We just need our funders to feel like it works.

In order to avoid any PII issues, following data collection we turned all our respondents into toads.
≠ Person
Therefore PII does not apply

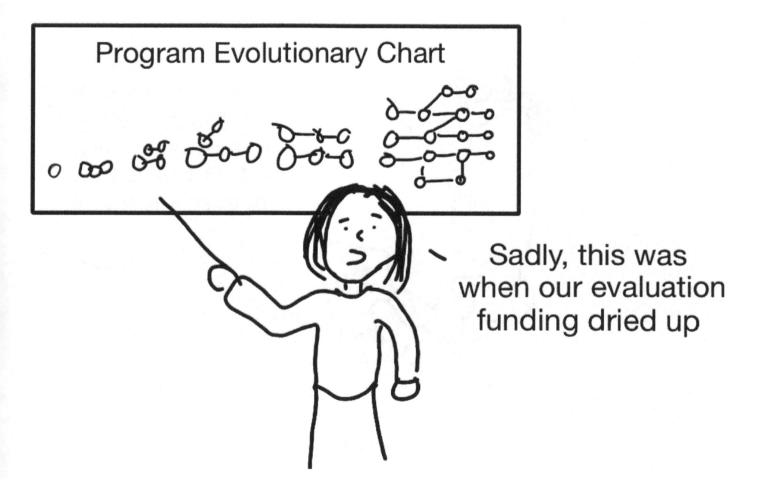

This report just says our project stinks!

That's a composite rating, my systematic assessment of every piece that stinks is in Appendix A

Nog call this Qualitative Data Visualization

According to our algorithm your daughter is at risk of failing 8th grade math.
But she's only in 5th grade!

Watson, I know what caused the death

But you have only administered a few interviews and gone on two site visits. Should you not collect evidence that is more robust?

I called you all here because
I need you to stop helping people.
It's really messing up my impact assessment.

In the red shorts we have one of the worst heavyweights in the WBA.
In the blue shorts, Jimmy, the best boxer in Ms. Templeton's fourth grade P.E. class.

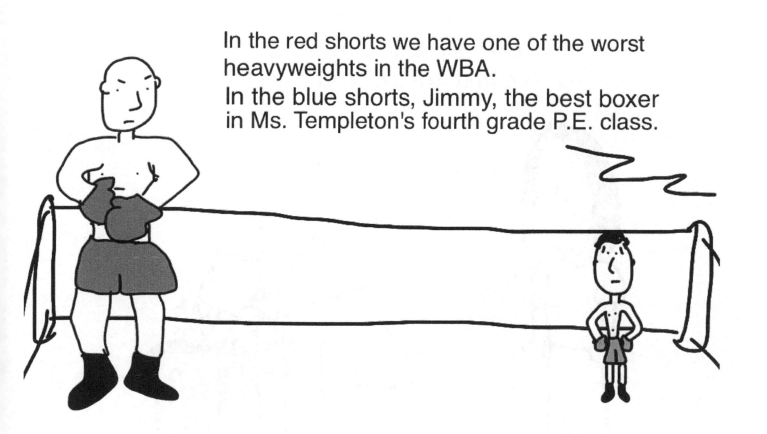

Those are good numbers.
Don't just throw them away.

It's far too complicated
to explain, so you'll
have to trust me.

But I don't
trust you.

This dashboard is
a solid first step.
Can the project team
suggest a few tweaks?

No, we could
barely afford the
initial development.

Write "reports" using "data"

Figure 1. How awesome we are

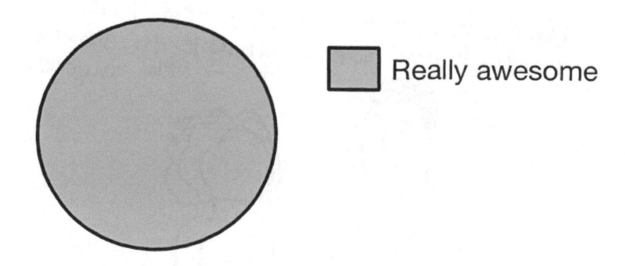

Really awesome

SOURCE: Because we said so

we spent the last 3 months writing the evaluation report.

Unfortunately we drained the budget and were unable to share it with anyone.

You say your program works but why should I believe you?

Because I have evidence.

Congressman,
there are other methods
that could provide some
useful evidence.

I don't need useful.

I need indisputable.

Daddy,
do you like
my picture?

Honey,
if you'd like me
to be objective,
I'll have to create
a rubric.

I value accuracy

More than you value your job?

Don't worry, the algorithm was designed to reflect our society. So it will only be racist and unjust if our society is racist and unjust.

Great news. RCT results are in, if the program is implemented with fidelity it produces significant results.

Cool, too bad it's impossible to implement.

We have a board meeting coming up and could use a little input from the evaluation team.

Sorry, we're not scheduled to provide input until year 3.

According to our evaluation. Jimmy's dad could most certainly beat up Tommy's dad.

Look everyone, Sarah thought it was OK to just color in the states!

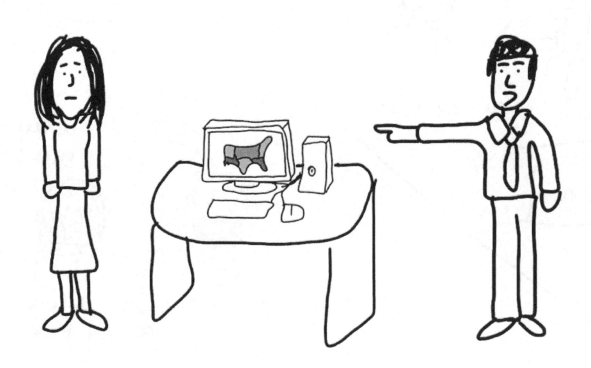

You've been given a great gift, George: A chance to see what the world would be like without you.

So like a really well designed counterfactual in an impact evaluation?

Hey guys,
did you read this part?

It basically says we
need an evaluation to
keep getting money.

I'm not a visual person.

So I will deliver my report in song,
hit it boys.

Why is the speedometer
stuck on 35?

The car only collects
speed data once
a year.

Well coding is free in that it only costs
years of experience and training.

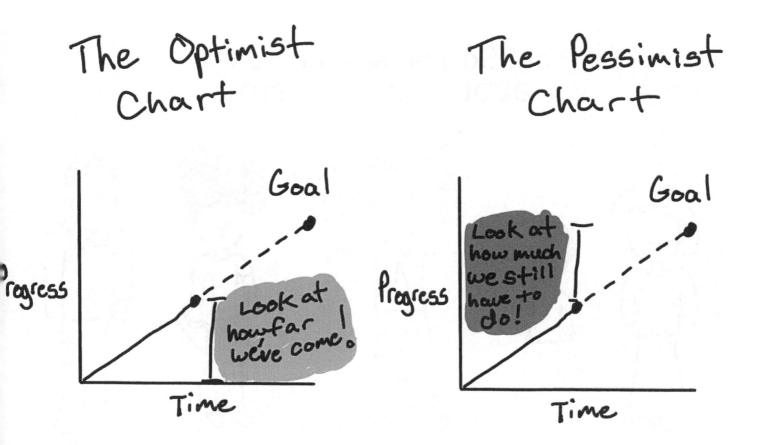

Every time I try to zoom in this happens...

Like I said before the paper is not interactive

Hello, you don't know or trust me, but can I ask you a bunch of deep probing questions about your work?

Why did you exclude all these responses?

We define outlier as someone who doesn't like our program

Formative, Summative, is that all you evaluators got?

Umm, well, umm how about dev-el-op-men-tal

Alright class, the end of year standardized testing is going to assess your creativity, ability to see humor, compassion for fellow human beings, empathy, critical thinking, and overall well-being.

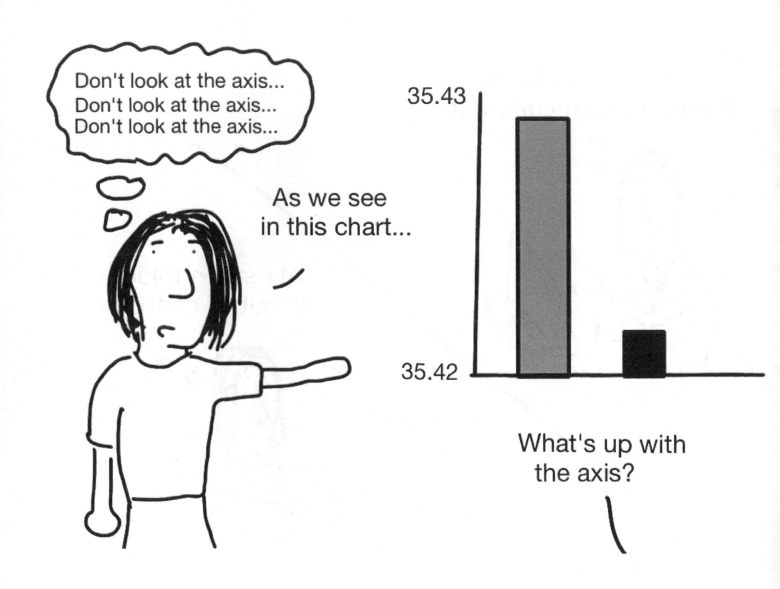

We got the report down
to 200 pages.

Awesome, so that's four
pages for each of our
50 unique audiences.

Congratulations Grads,
after you pick up your diploma
go ahead and drop your dissertation
into the bottomless pit to my left.

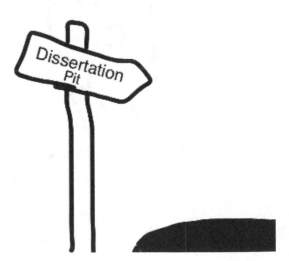

Dissertation
Pit

I'm all for gamechangers
but now everyone's
playing a different game?

So our design approach relies on quick prototypes, user feedback, and lots of iterations.

Our evaluation approach forces you to quit doing any of that.

well first, I want to thank you all for joining me as we kick off our evaluation.

I'll be assigning textbooks based on your evaluation personalities. Show of hands, any realist participatory systems change modelers? How about collaborative new age randomistas?

Like an evaluator in a data store

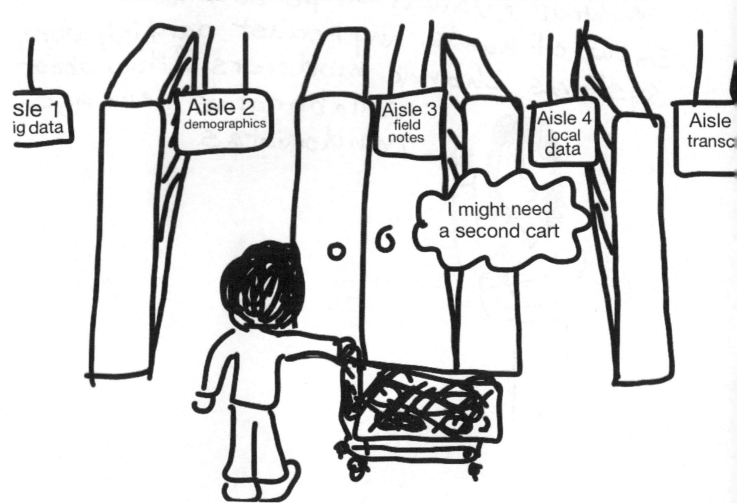

It makes sense.
I just don't care.

In order to avoid any PII issues, we published it to a part of the web where it will most likely never be seen. You know, fingers crossed.

Somewhere, at this very moment...

30 revisions,
are you a
perfectionist?

No, I'm just stuck
in a formative
self-evaluation
feedback loop.

Well RCTs are
the gold standard.

They're like a shiny rock
that only has value
because people with a
vested interest say so?

Grant Evaluation Lifecycle

What they don't teach you in grad school

By the time the data is ready for publication
you will despise it

According to the RFP, the annual report should be under 700 characters and delivered in 5 tweets.

In order to reach all of our diverse audiences, the final report is now 17,000 pages.

You can pick it up here. hand-trucks are available at the back of the room.

We're just starting to plan our evaluation. Which methods should we consider?

All of them.

Social Network
Analysts

Antisocial
Network
Analyst

We did it!

We saved the
children?

No, 1 million
views on YouTube!

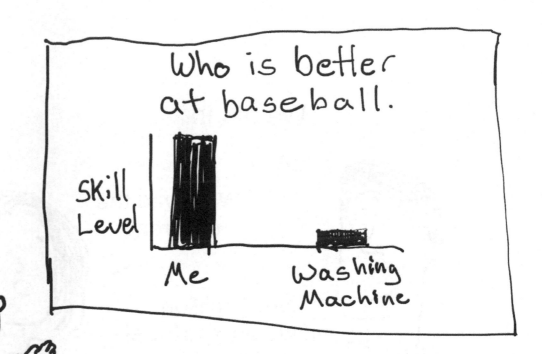

As you can all see from this chart, I am awesome at baseball.

Did you bedazzle all of
your charts?

Fancy, right?

Congratulations everyone! Thanks to our program unemployment is down.

But those numbers were collected before our program was even launched.

According to our
Study, when human
teeth fall out, they
are replaced by bigger
stronger teeth.

Was your sample
composed entirely of
young children

How did you know?

Our program's goal is to make your live's better, as defined by the 10 old white guys on our foundation's board.

Truth in Presentation Design

I added the references to make my BS seem well researched —

• I am awesome

Terwilliger, Donrun, and Joseph. 2009. "Monekys and their poo."
Jungle Press. Tuscon

Terwilliger and Joseph. 2007. "Oof that hurt my head."
BS Press. Nowheresville

Tankerton. 2012. Boo, ha scared you.
Taneytown press. Taneytown

Sandddd. 1999. "I'm sad because my name has too many ds."
Kermie Unlimited. Sesame

Bollards. 2011. "No it's not a curse word."
BS Press. Nowheresville

I just put our long boring report up on a buried web page in a format that requires it to be downloaded. Yet for some reason, nobody is reading it.

Information Overload

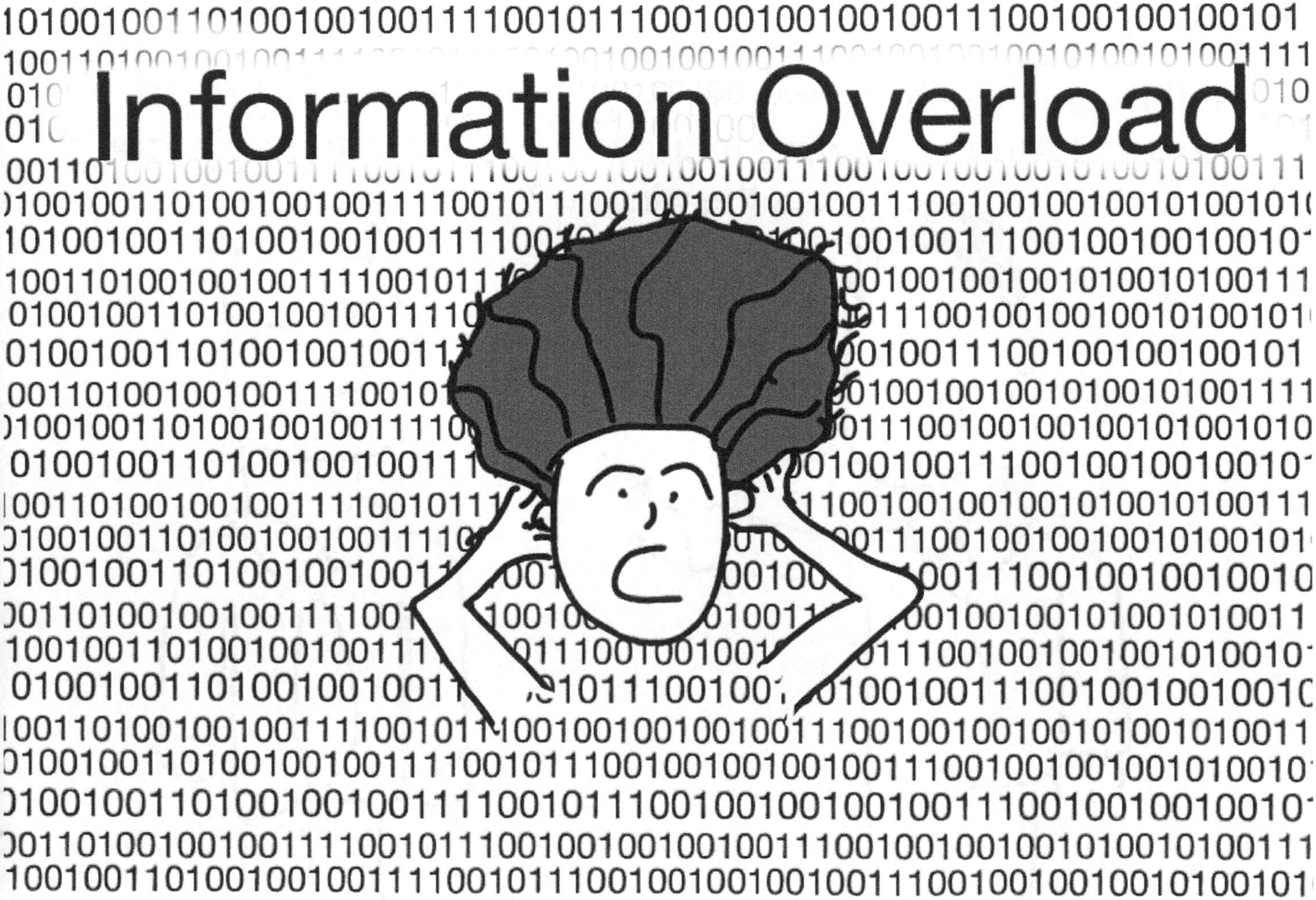

We surveyed our 3 program participants...

% who think we're awesome

100%

What about the 96 families that left after the first week?

Wyoming

DC

With your ongoing support
we can make this evaluation
a success.

Collaborative

Working together, we will
make this evaluation a success.

Participatory

We'll have help, but the success
of the evaluation is in our hands.

Empowerment

Bar Chart

Column Chart

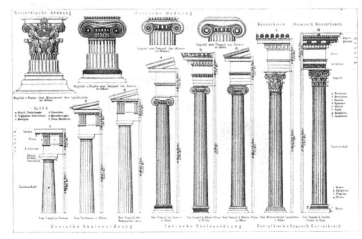

Dear Parents,
To show our commitment to evidence-based practice, this year's fourth grade class will be randomly assigned to one of two groups.
The treatment group will receive a good education while the control group will receive a placebo. This study will provide value for generations to come.

Can you describe how
the program is doing?

No, but I can give you
some numbers based
on crazy assumptions
and lots of big data.

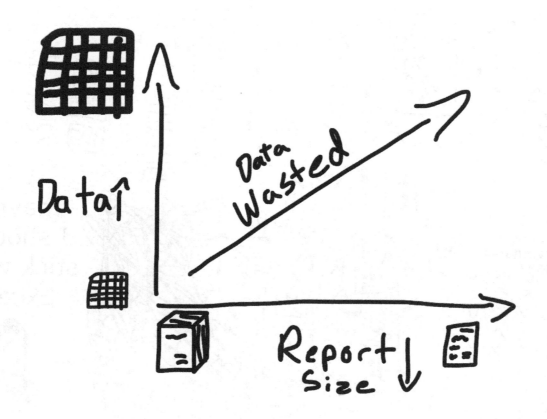

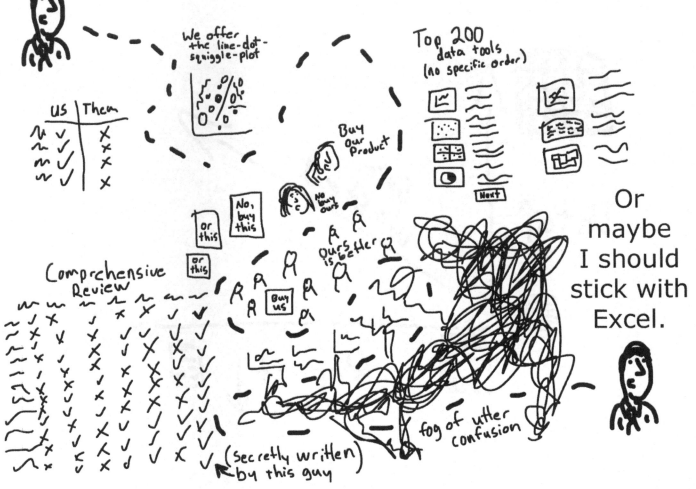

I'm beginning to think that the higher death rate in black communities might have a lot to do with social and economic factors.

Really? People should hear about that. You should write a paper.

The Negro death rate and sickness are largely matters of condition and not due to racial traits and tendencies... 1906

W.E.B. Du Bois

As you all know, this leadership team has been facing some criticism for our total lack of diversity. Since equity is one of our core values we have decided to create a space on our team for one person of color to be hired into leadership in the coming year.

Hey, you with the survey! Quit collecting data, it's getting in the way of our doing stuff!

What floor?

Oh, hey, you're black.

Let me ask you something.
Wouldn't it make sense to just tackle poverty?

All this focus on racism but isn't the problem really just income inequality?
Poor blacks, poor whites, what's the difference?

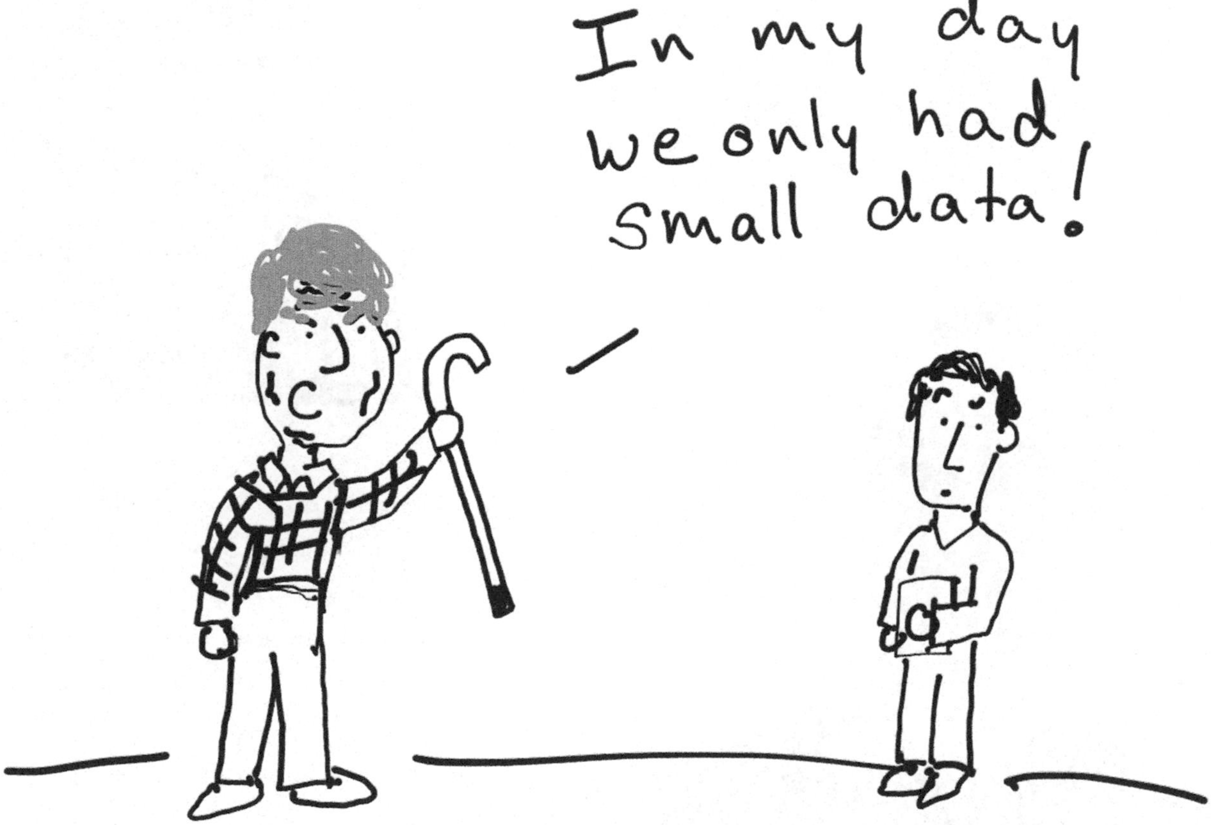
In my day we only had small data!

MY NAME IS CHRIS LYSY

I draw cartoons as a way to explore ideas, focus my mind, and channel my curiosity. And for close to a decade I have shared my work openly through my blog at freshspectrum.com.

Over time it found an audience, and my creations have appeared in thousands of presentations, social media posts, and influential textbooks.

This is my first stand-alone cartoon book.

Made in the USA
Monee, IL
13 September 2020